Raven's Li'l Critters

Raven's Li'l Critters

by
Raven OKeefe

A Black Coat Press Book

Copyright © 2008 by Raven OKeefe.

Visit the artist's websites:
http://www.ravenokeefe.com
Horse portraits:
http://www.ravenshorses.com
Faithful friends portraits:
http://www.faithfulfriendsportraits.com
L'il Critters:
http://ravenslilcritters.com
Wool Sculpture:
http://www.woolsculpture.com
Wildlife & Fine Art:
http://www.artbyraven.com
Border Collies Art:
http://www.bcstyleyes.com
http://www.canismajorart.com

To contact Raven OKeefe:
e-mail: portraits@ravenokeefe.com
post: 39562 Highway 226, Scio, OR 97374.

Visit our website at www.blackcoatpress.com

ISBN 978-1-934543-62-7. First Printing December 2008. Published by Black Coat Press, an imprint of Hollywood Comics.com, LLC, P.O. Box 17270, Encino, CA 91416. All rights reserved. Except for review purposes, no part of this book may be reproduced or transmitted in any form or by any means, electronic or mechanical, including photocopying, recording, or by any information storage and retrieval system, without permission in writing from the artist or the publisher. Printed in the United States of America.

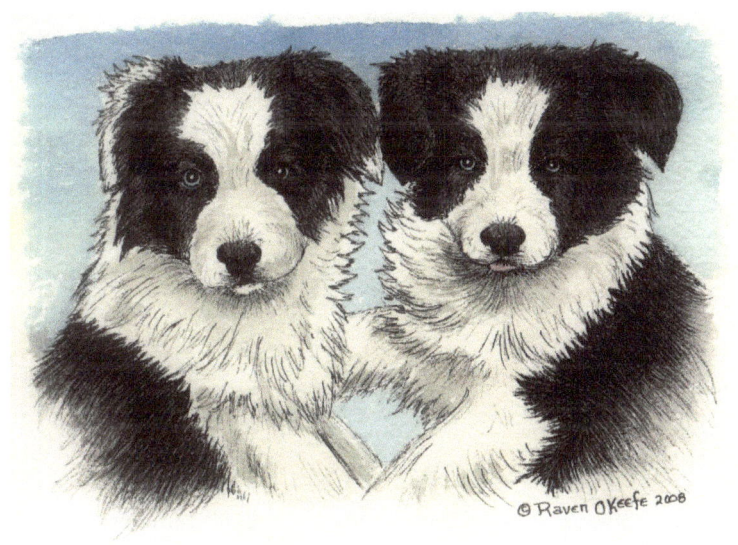

Ain't we cute?

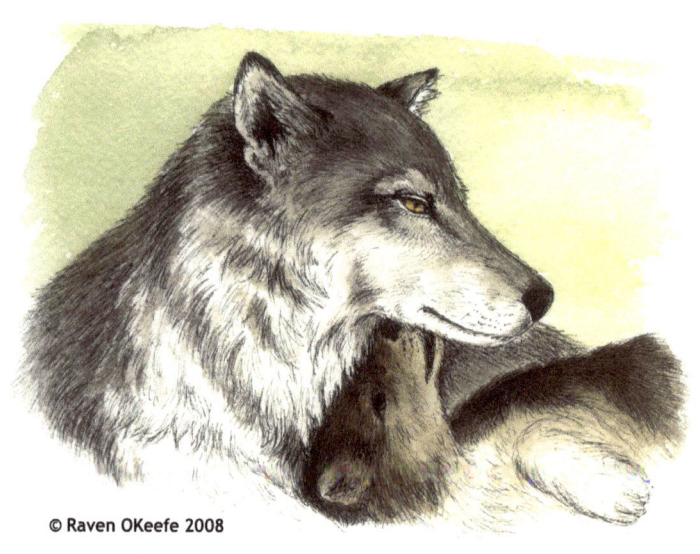

Alpha someday...

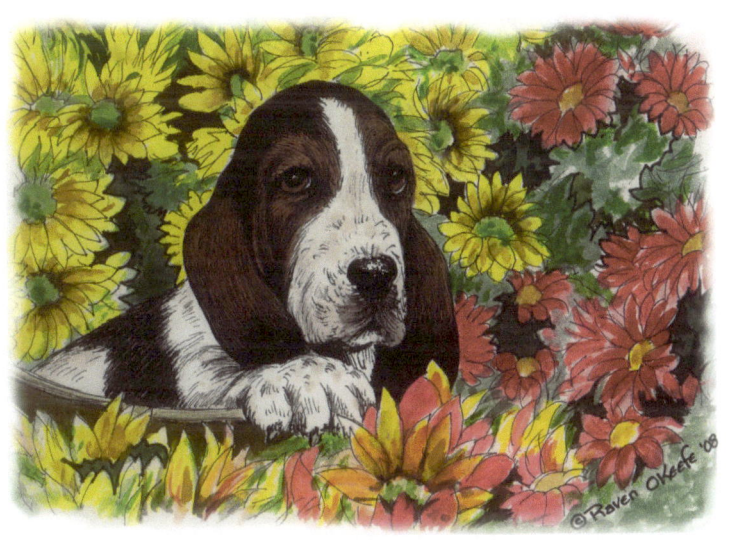

Am I a flower?

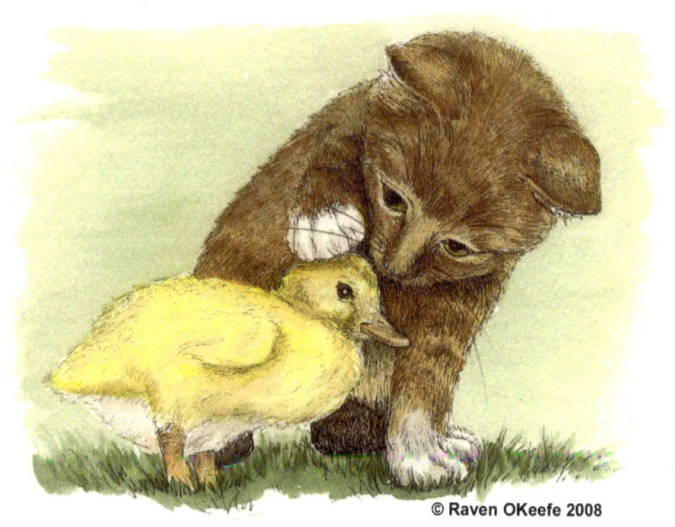

Awww... Soft

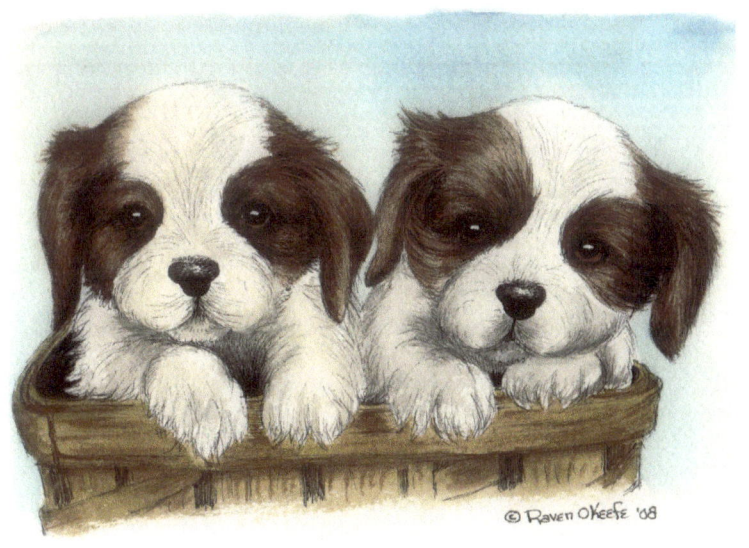

Basket Cases

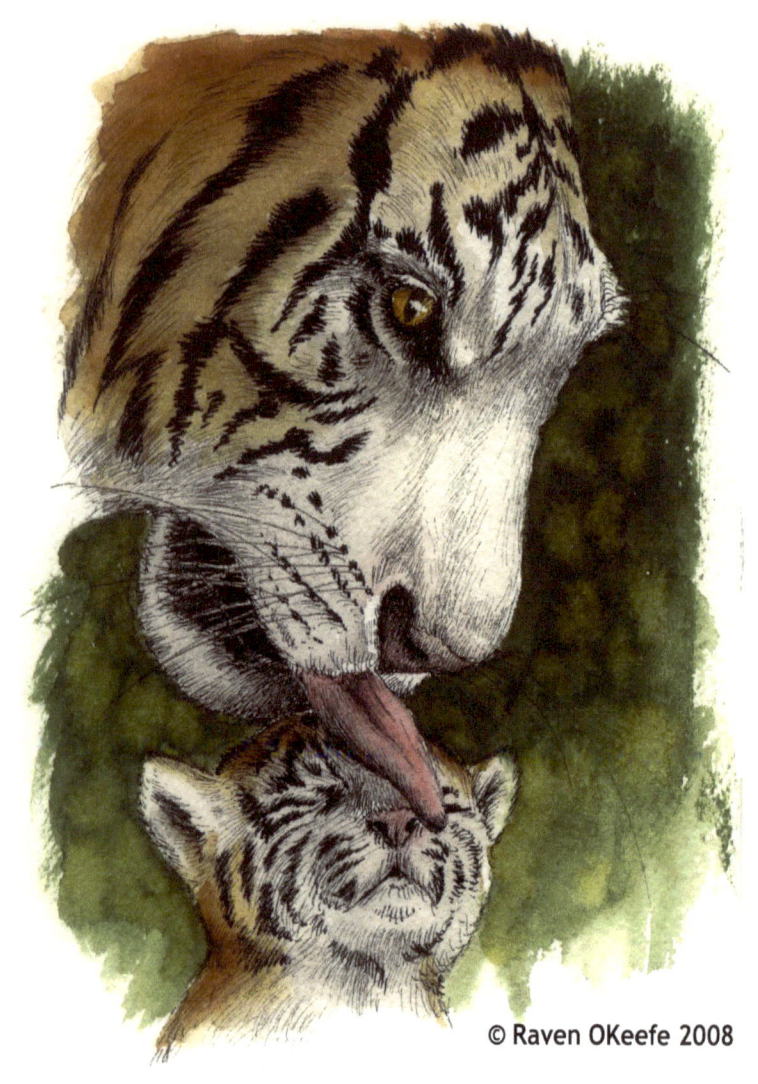

Bath Time

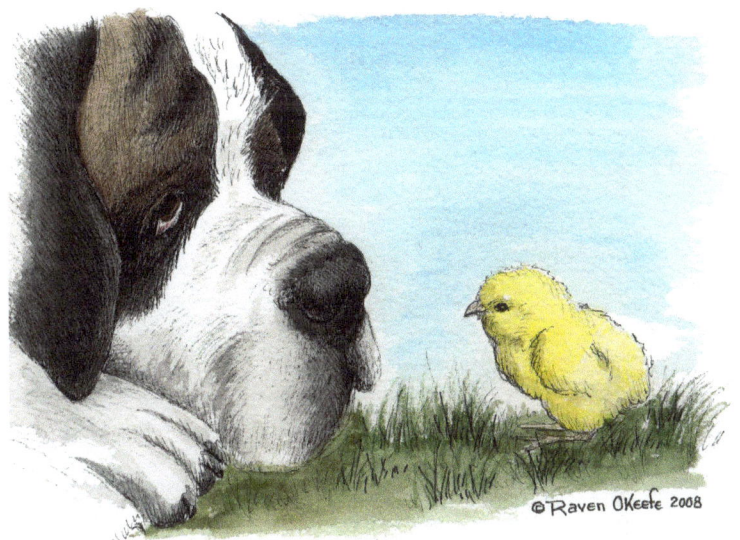

Big and Little

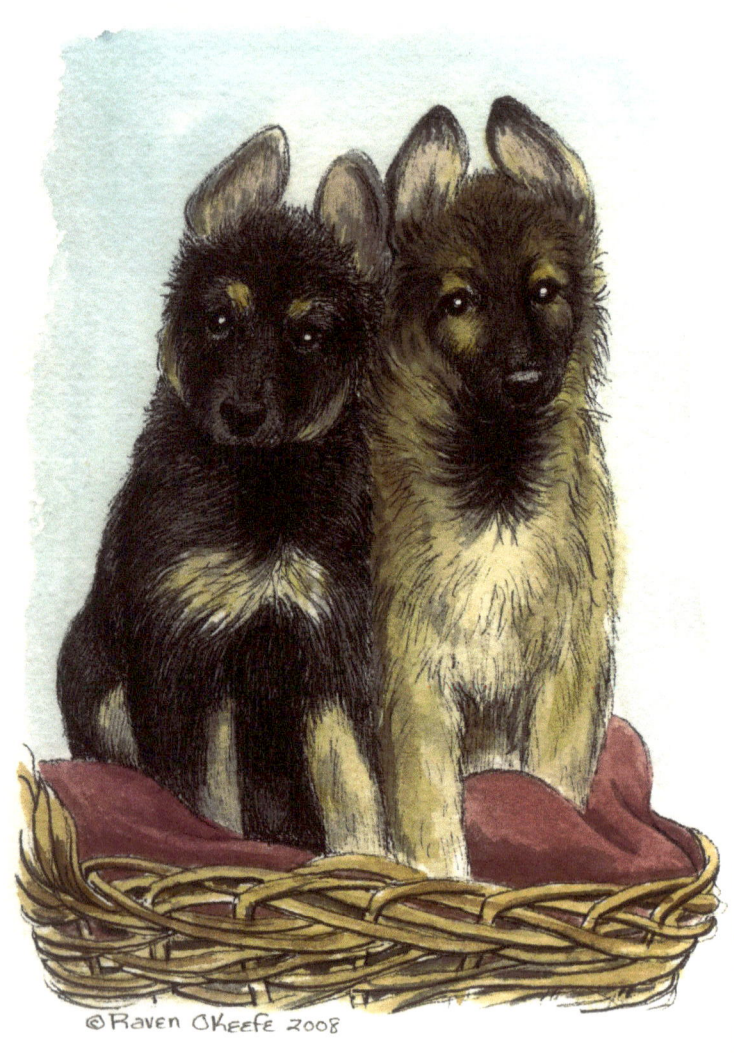

Brothers

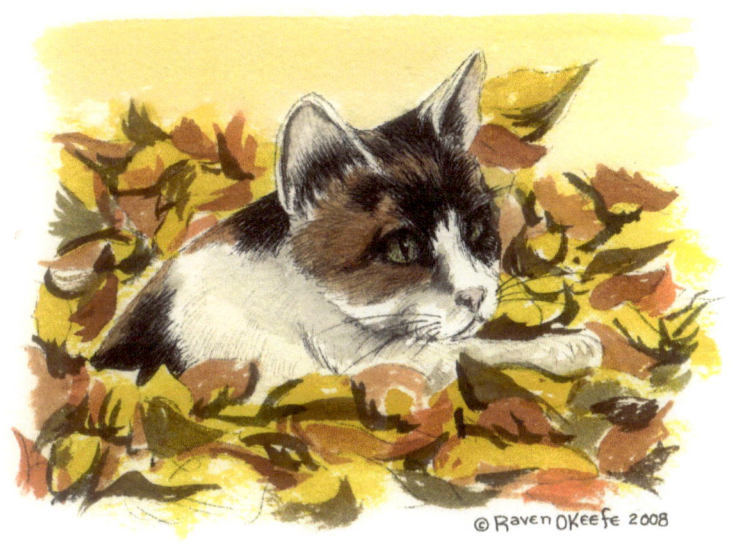

Camouflage

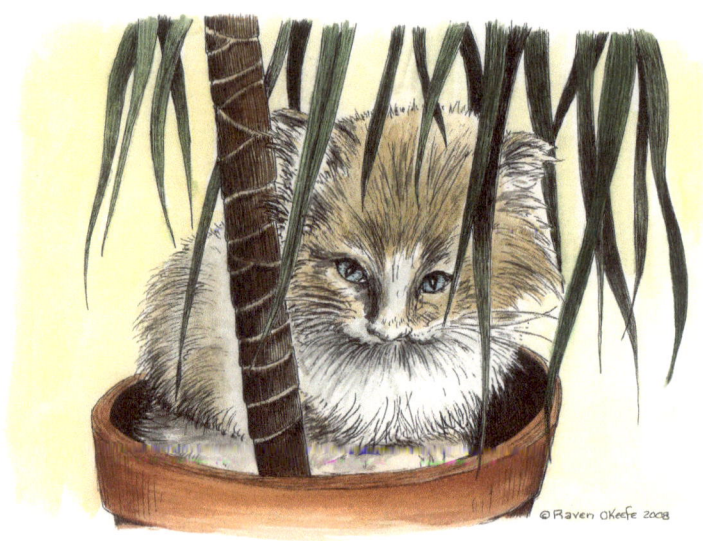

Can't see me!

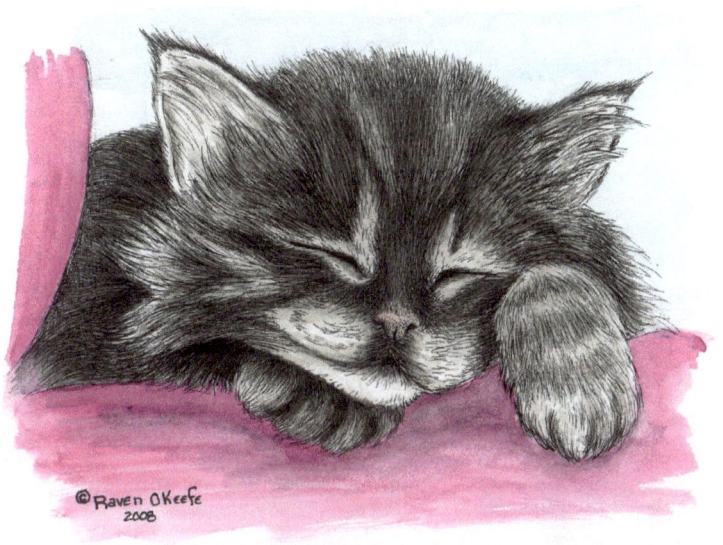

Cat Nap

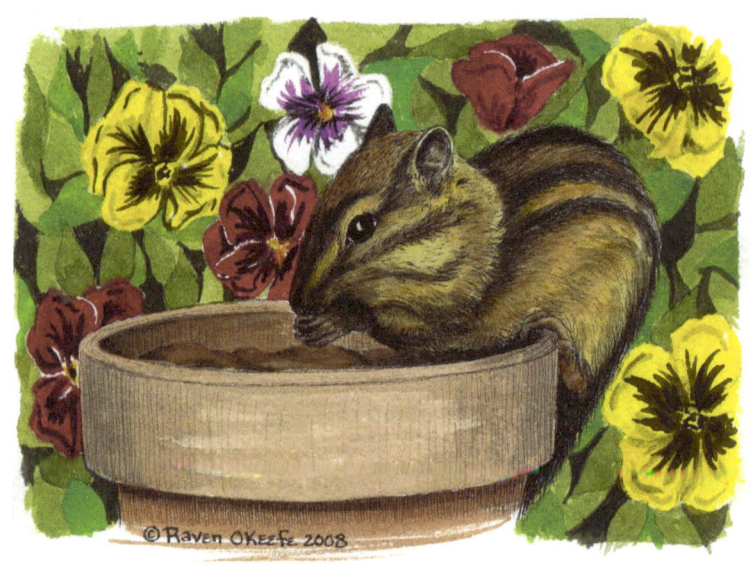

Chippie

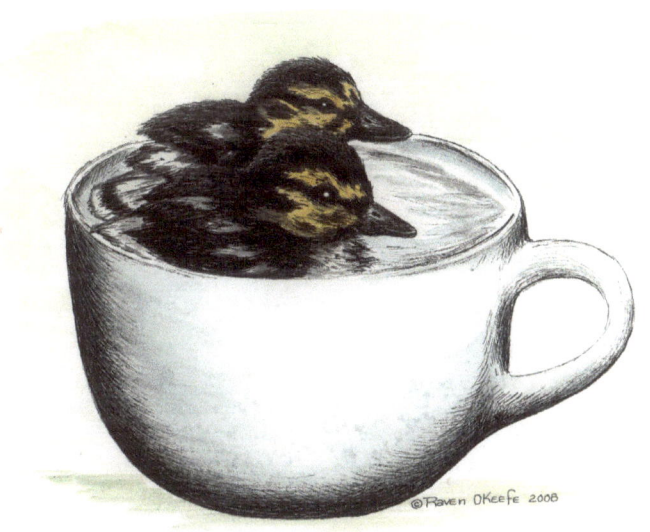

Cup o'Ducks

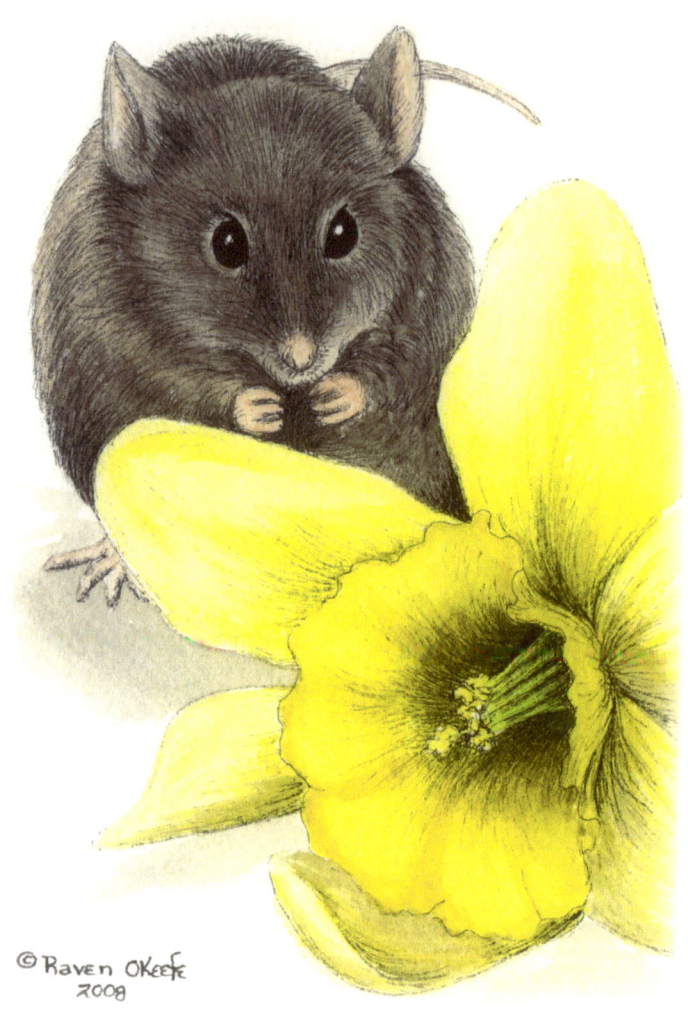

Daffy

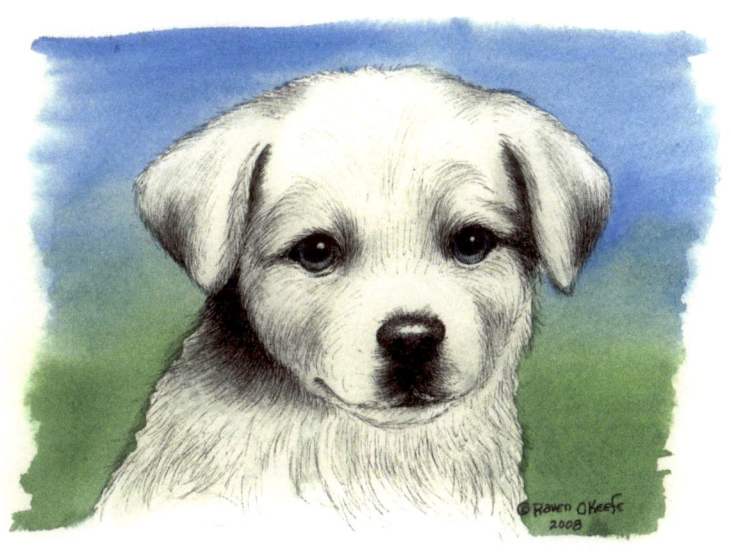

Don't call me cute!

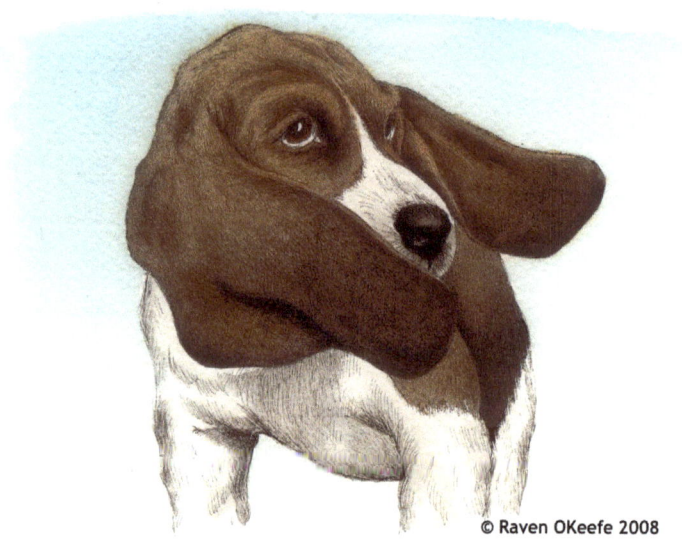

Don't need a weatherman

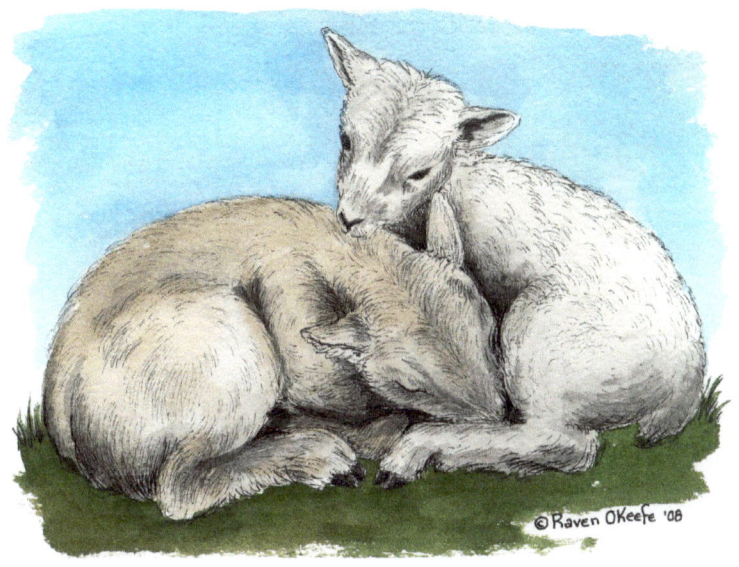

Eggshell and Ecru

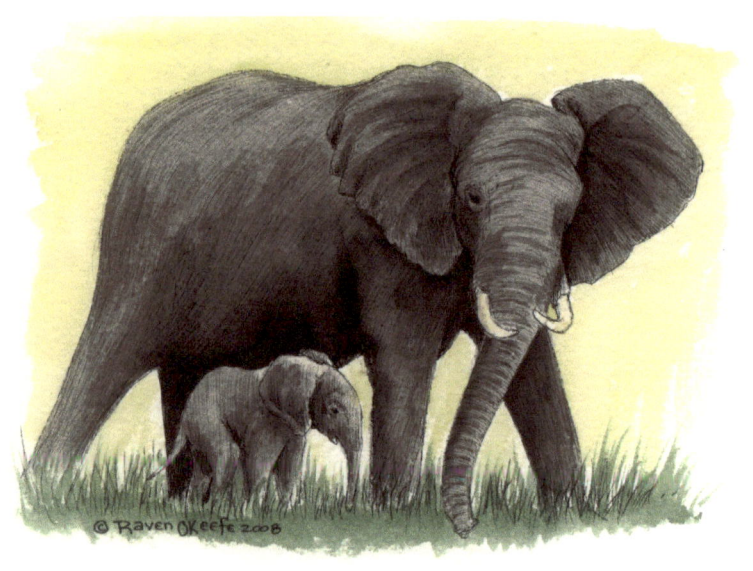

Ellie Mae

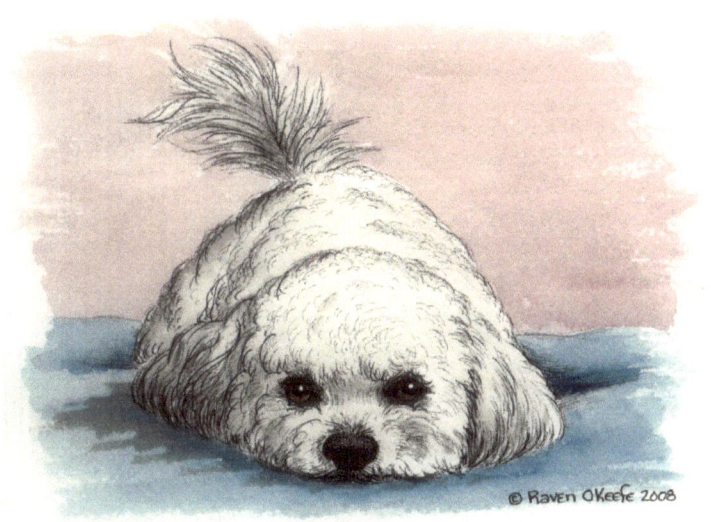

Fluffy

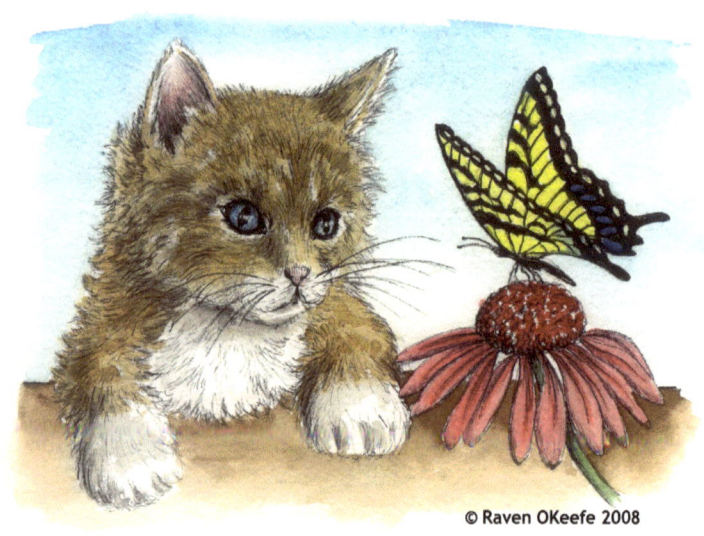

Flutterby

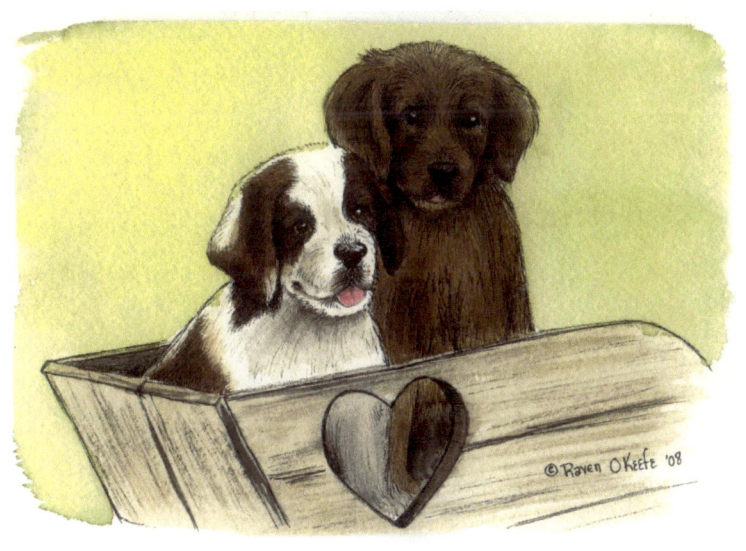

Heart to Heart

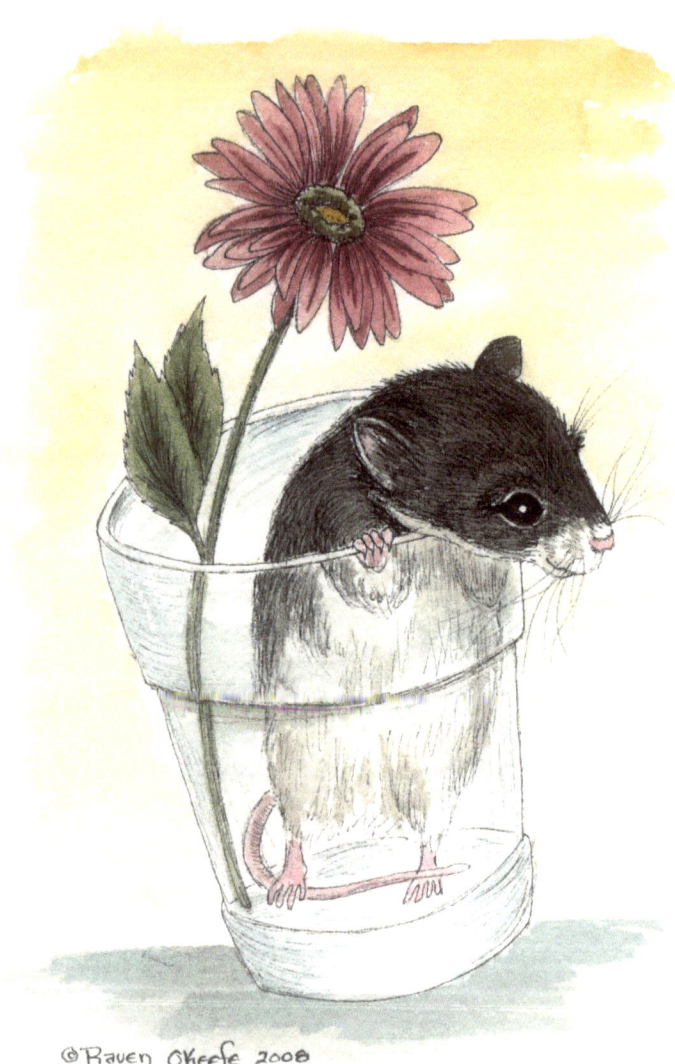

I can explain

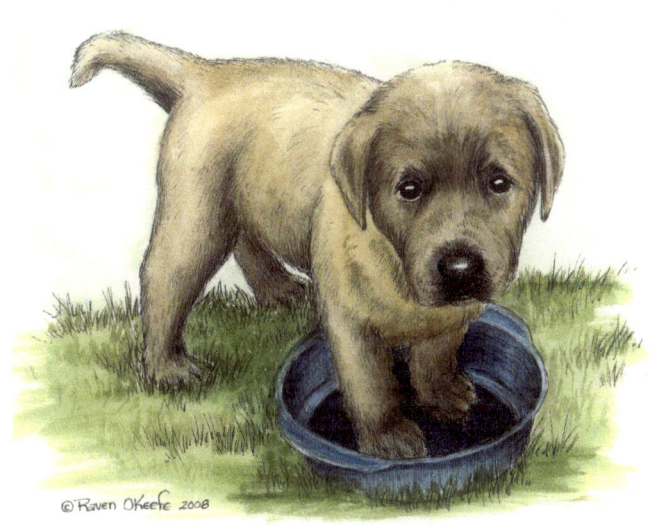

It's Supper Time!

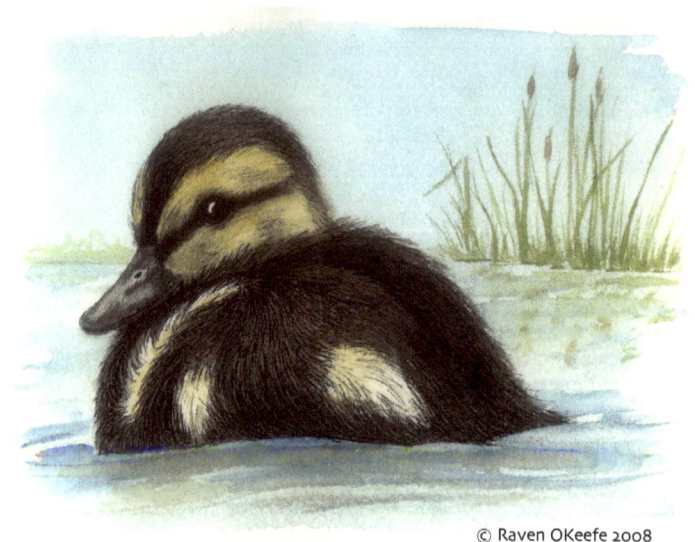

Just Ducky

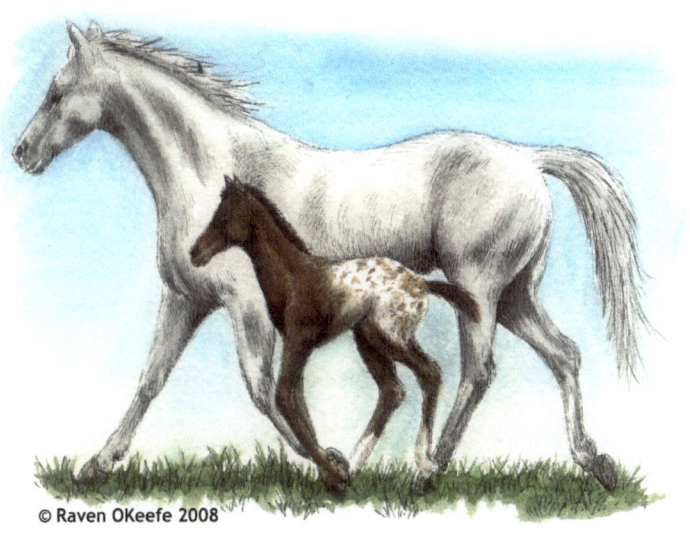

Keep up

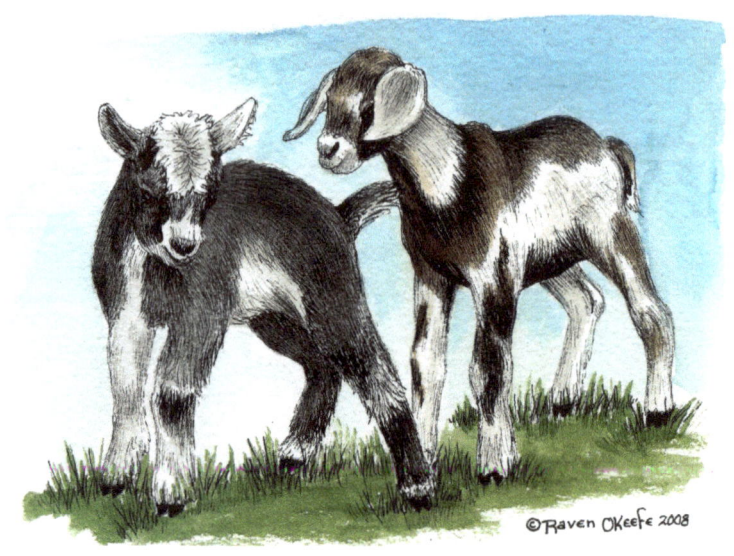

Kidz 'n the 'Hood

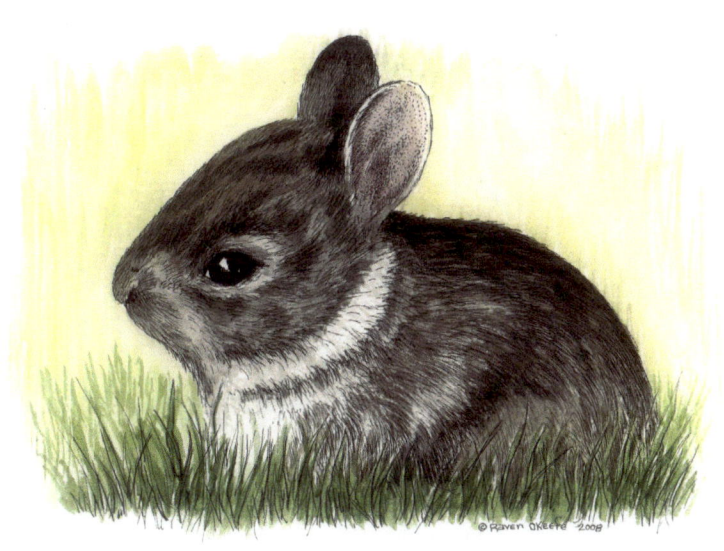

L'il Bun

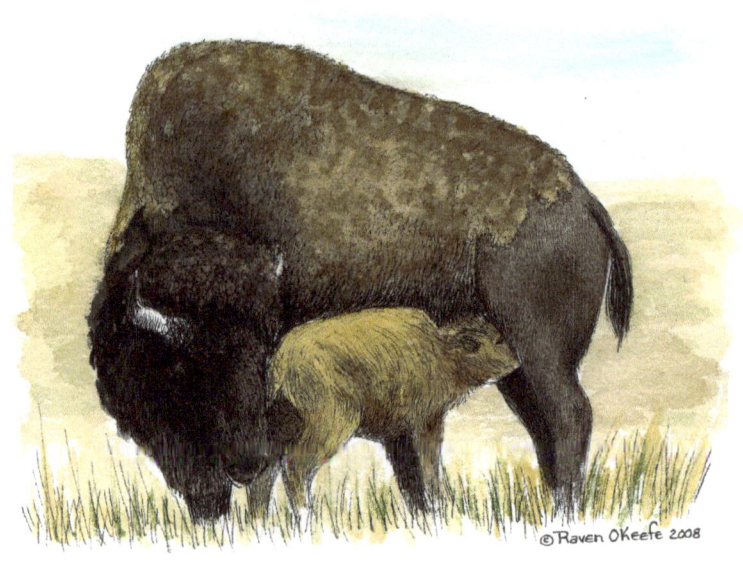

Little Tatanka

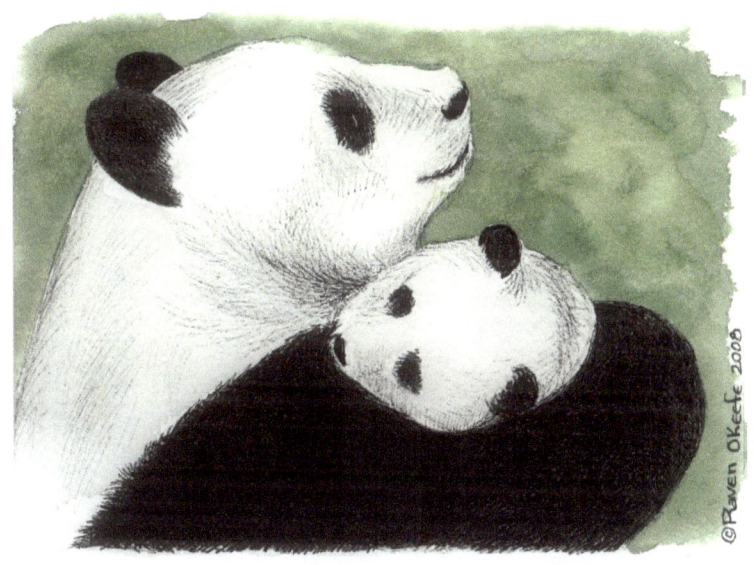

Lullaby

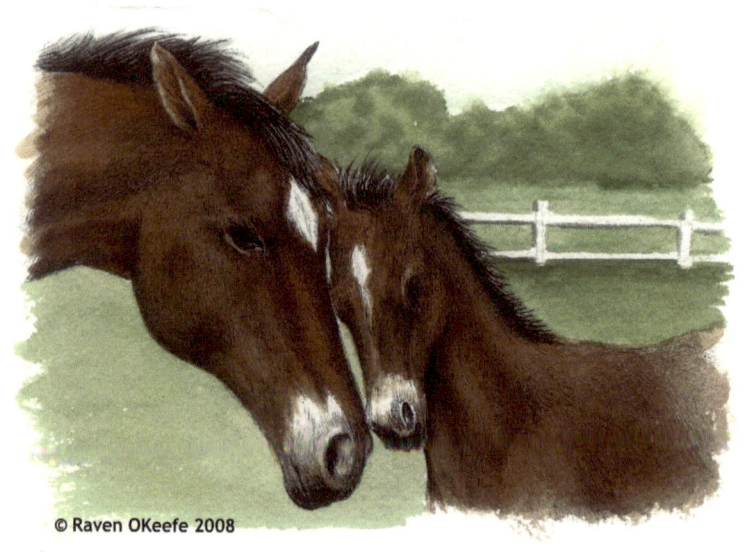

Me and Mom

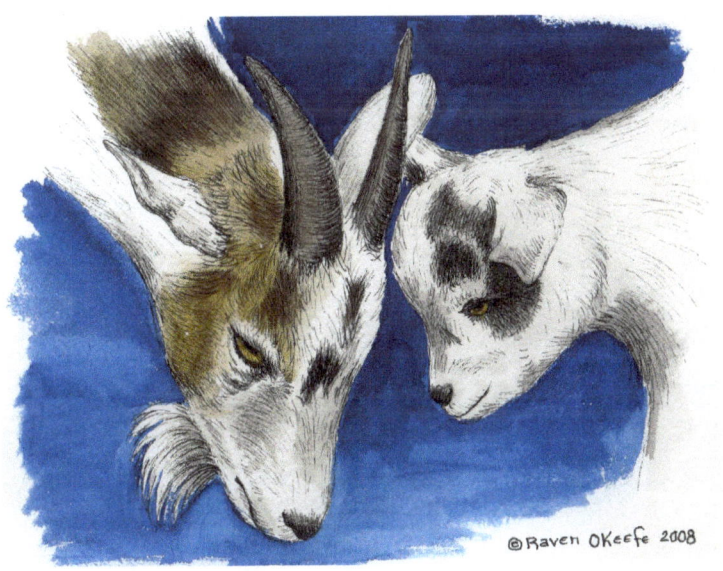

Me and My Kid

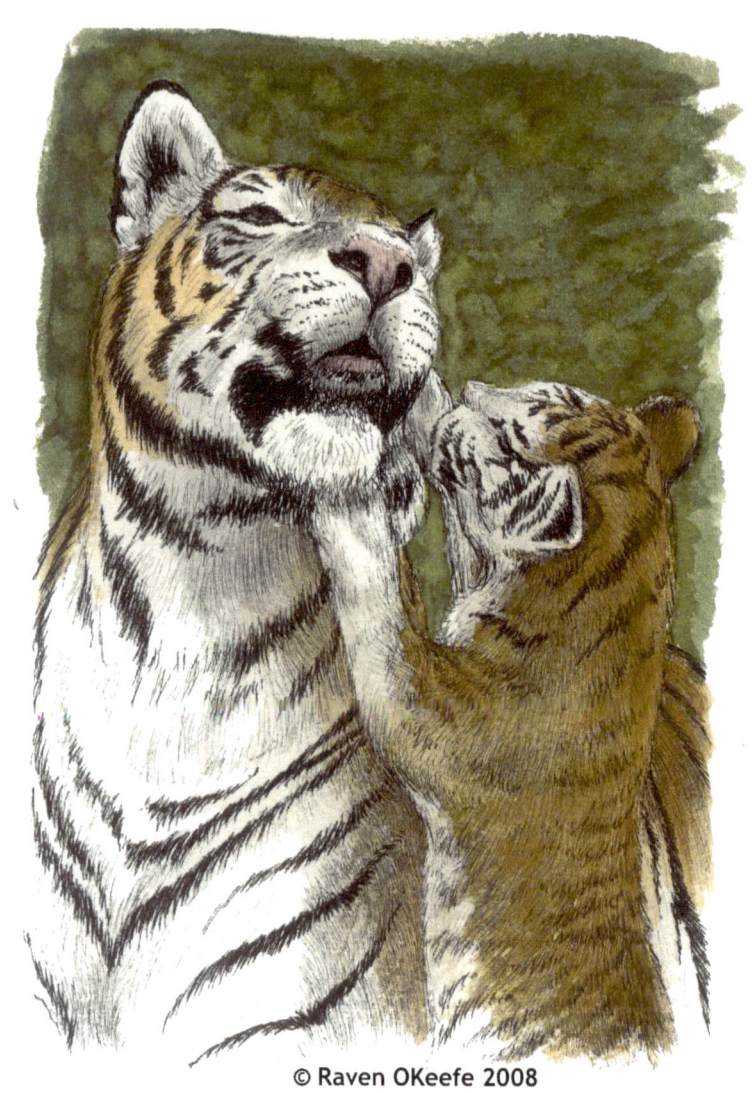

Mom, Hey Mom!

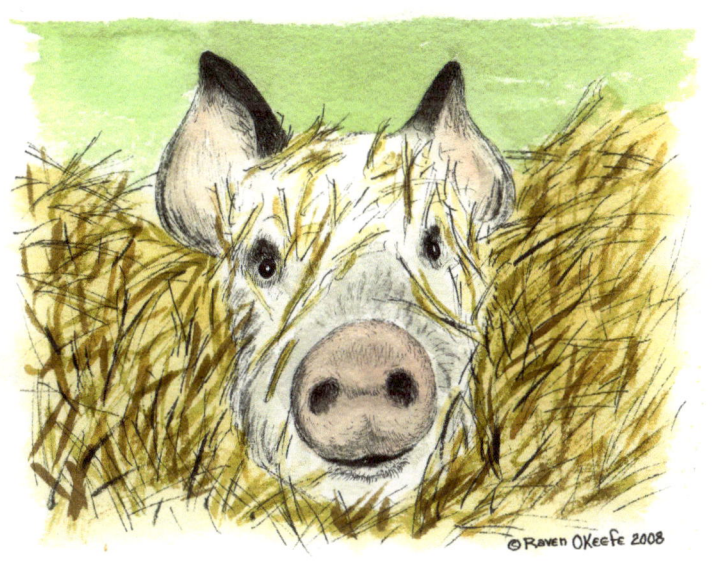

Needle

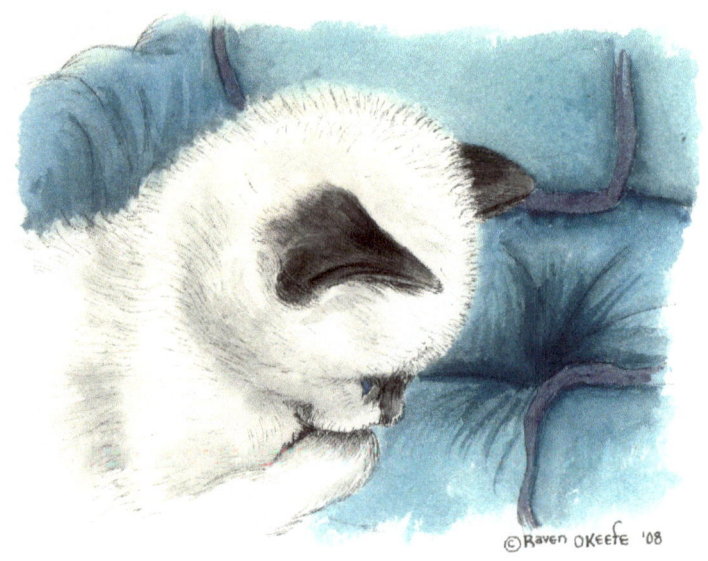

Now I lay me

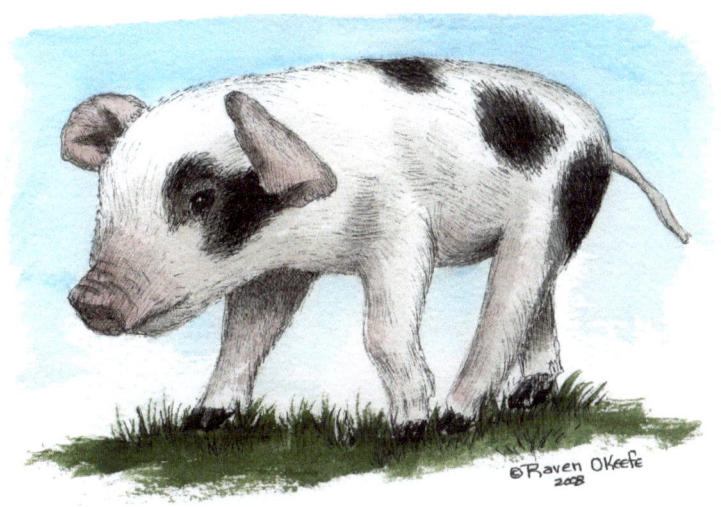

Oink

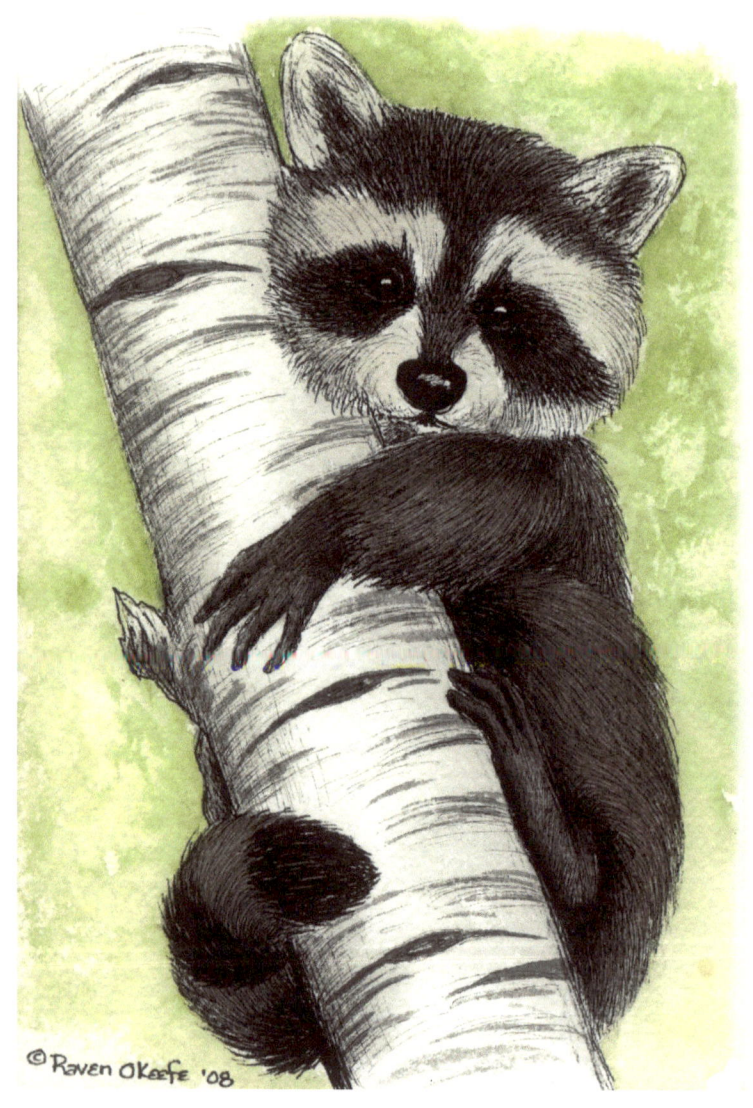

Oops!

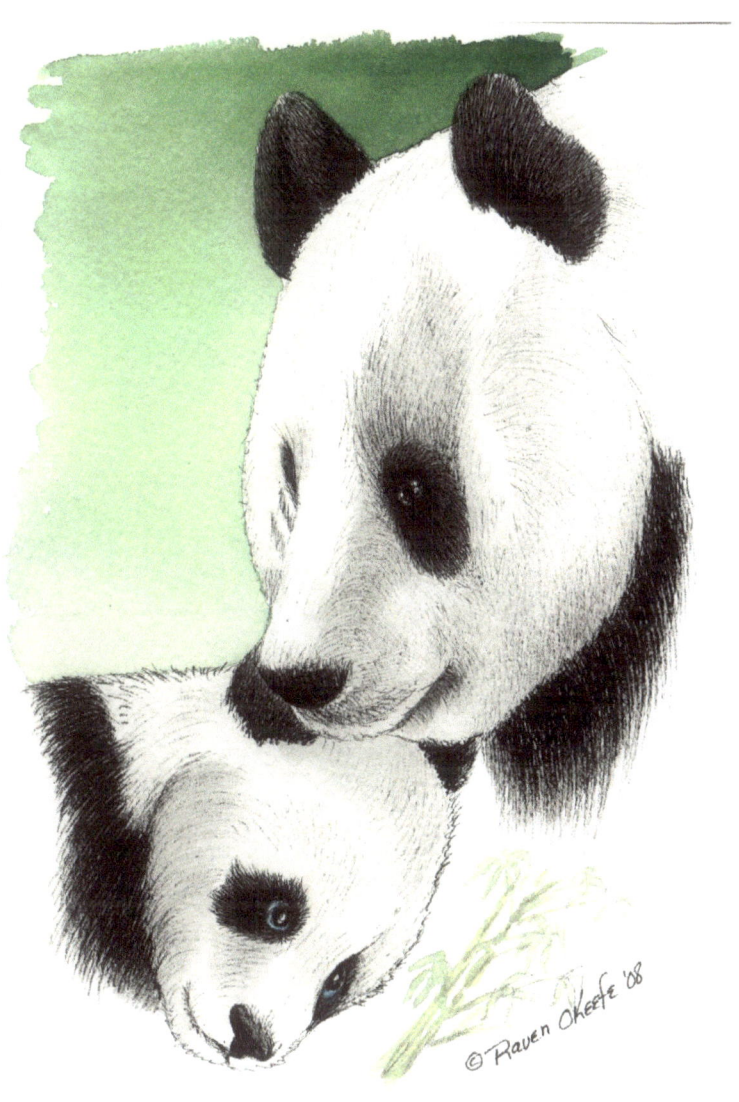

Panda-monium

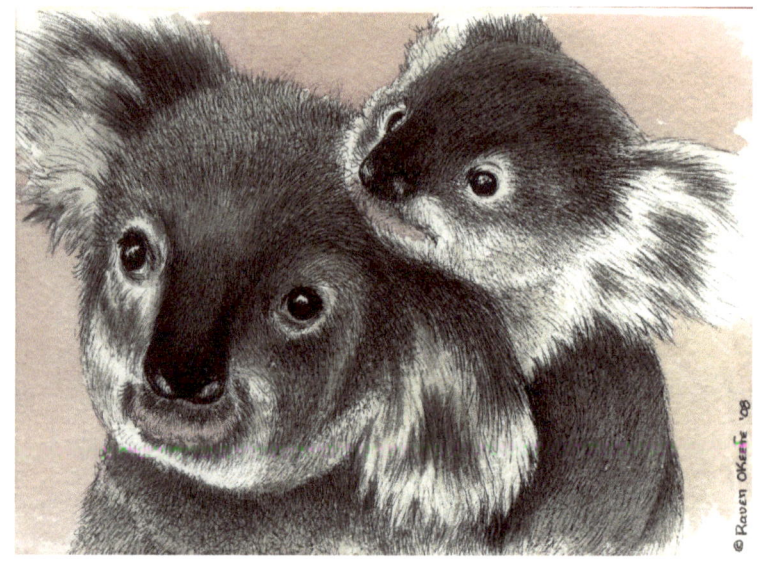

Peekaboo

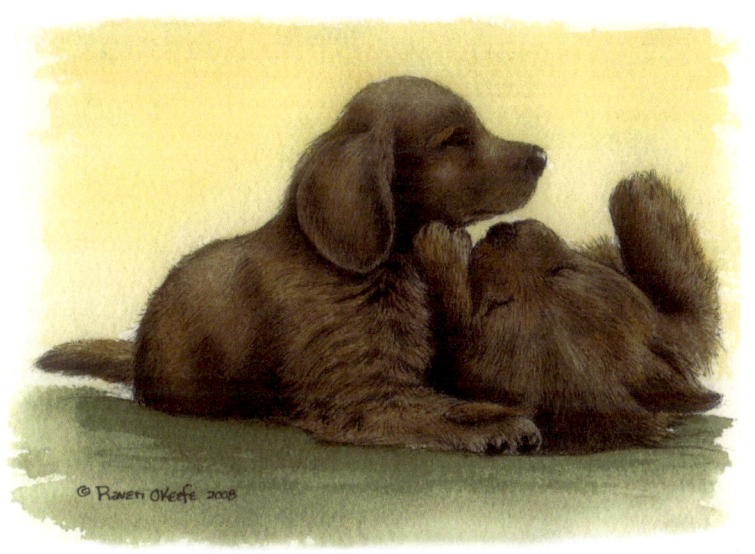

Play with me

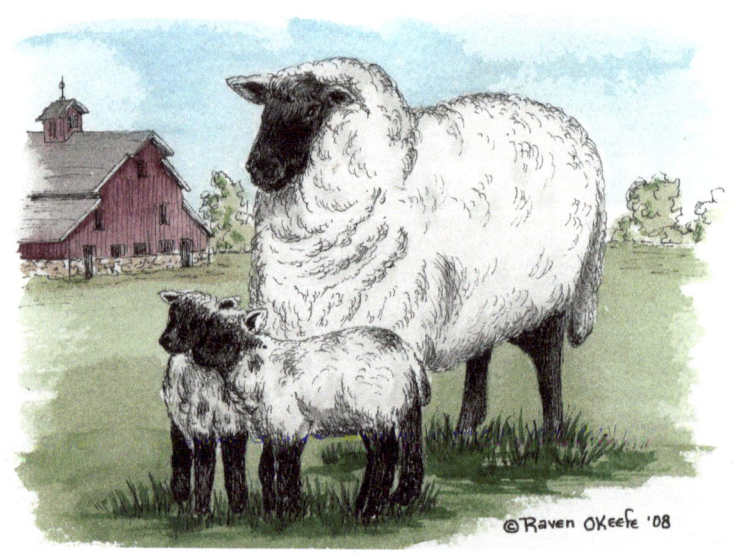

Proud Mama

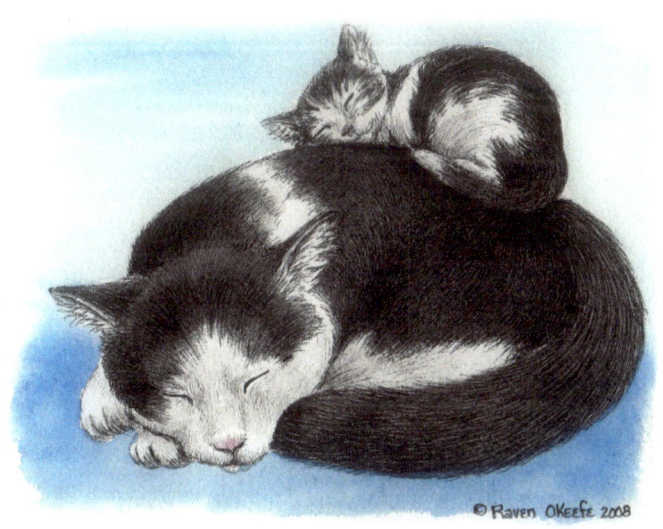

Purr-fect Sleeper

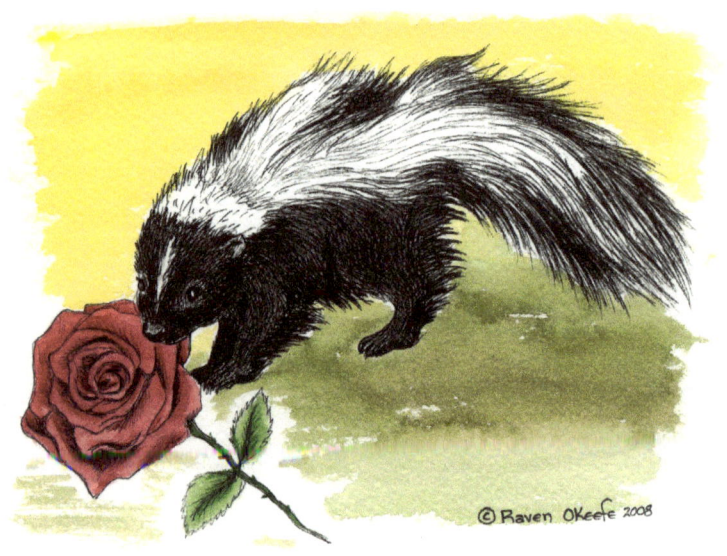

Rosie

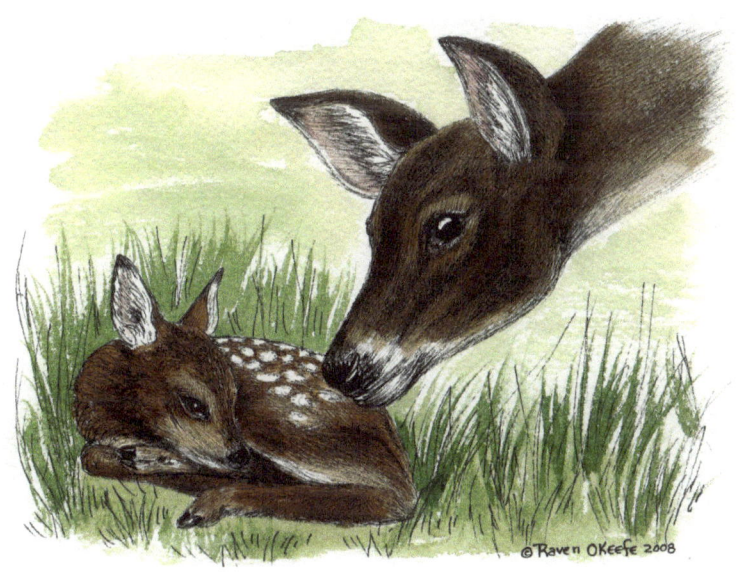

Safe Little One

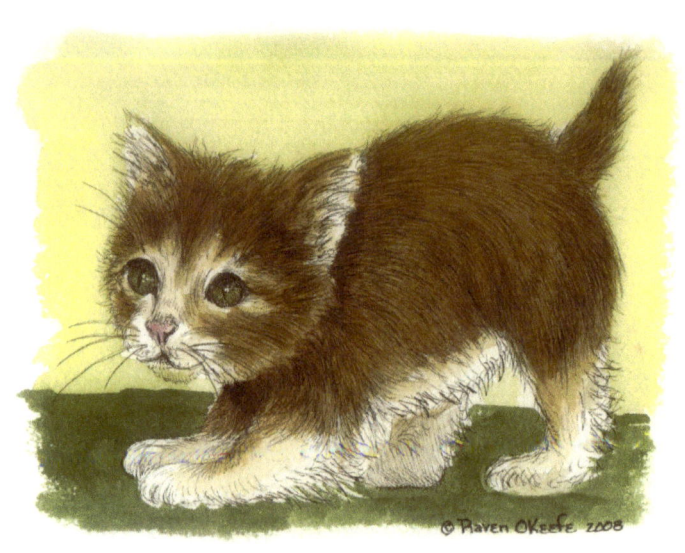

Scruffy

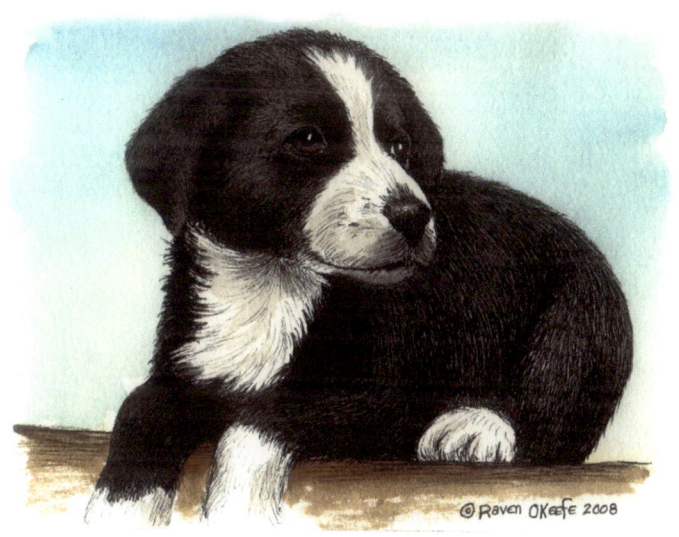

Sheep in my future

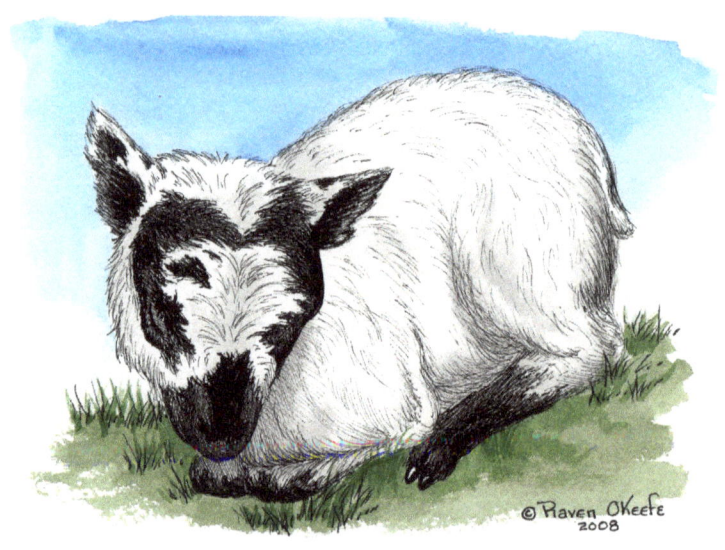

Sleepy Lambie

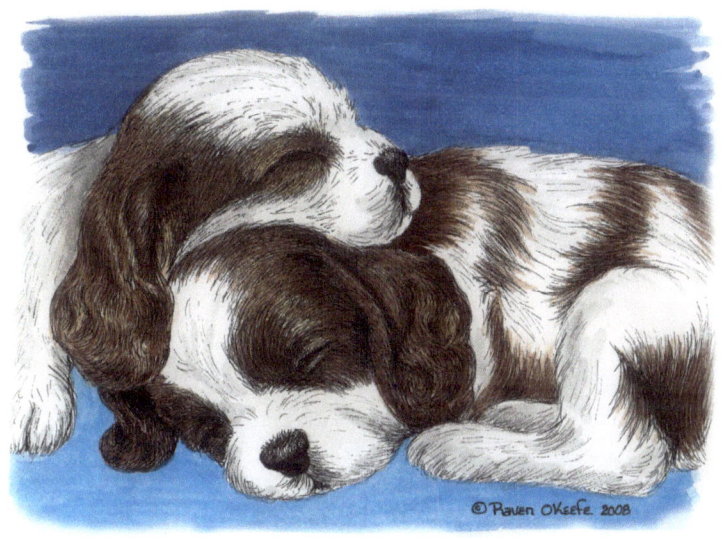

Snoozin'

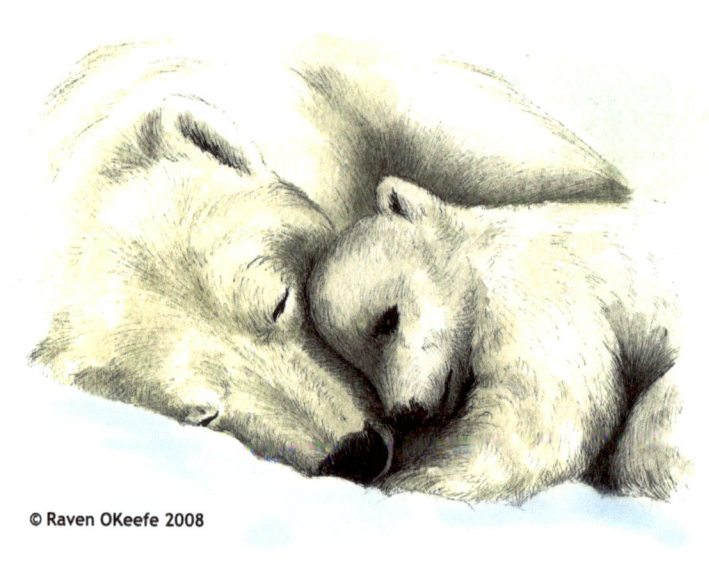

Snowy snooze

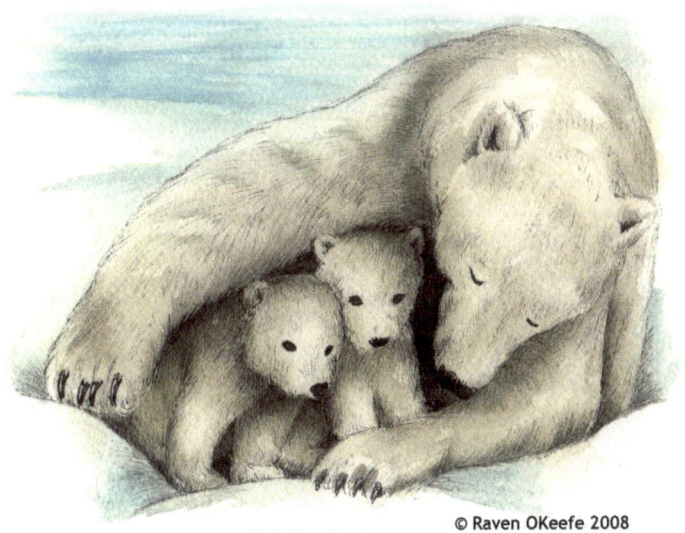

Snuggle up

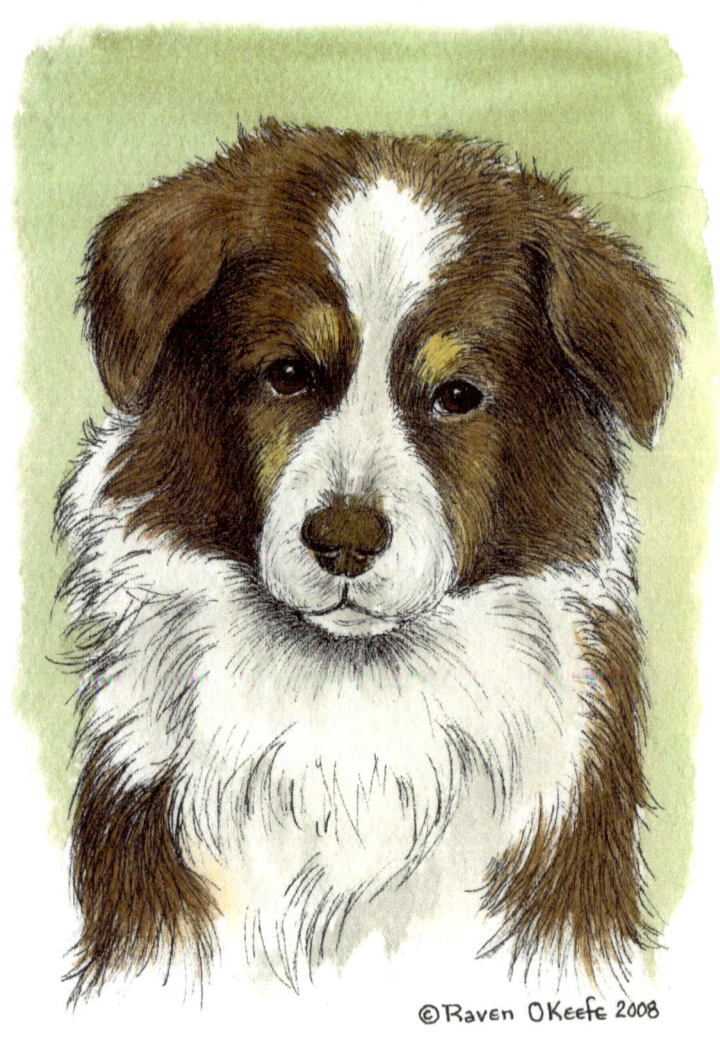

Strawberry Blonde

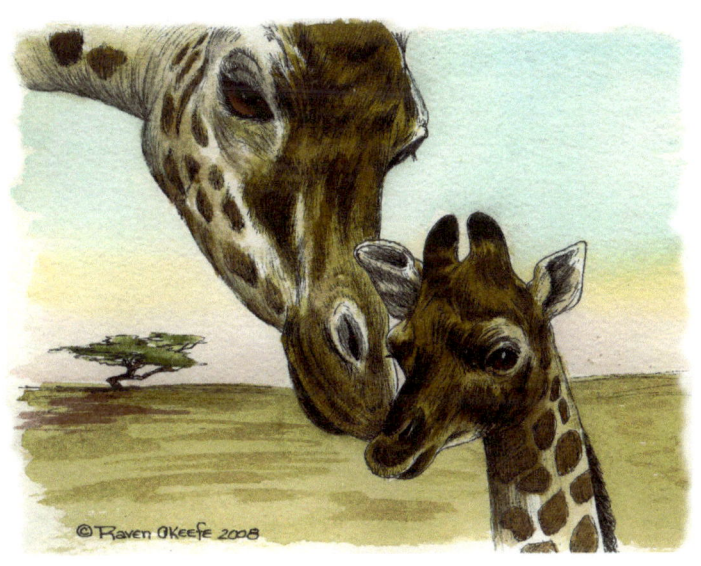

Tall Tails

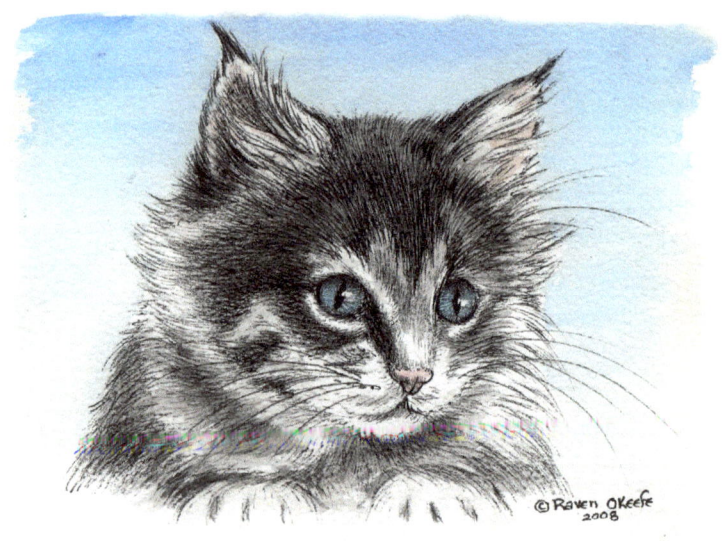

Whiskers

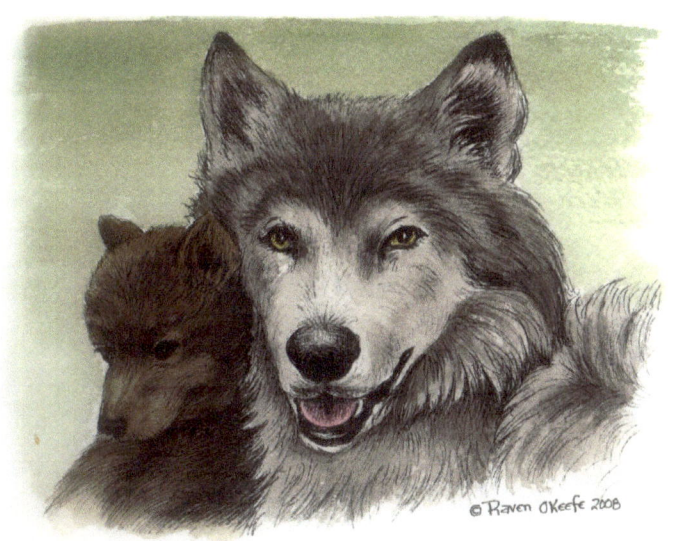

Woof!

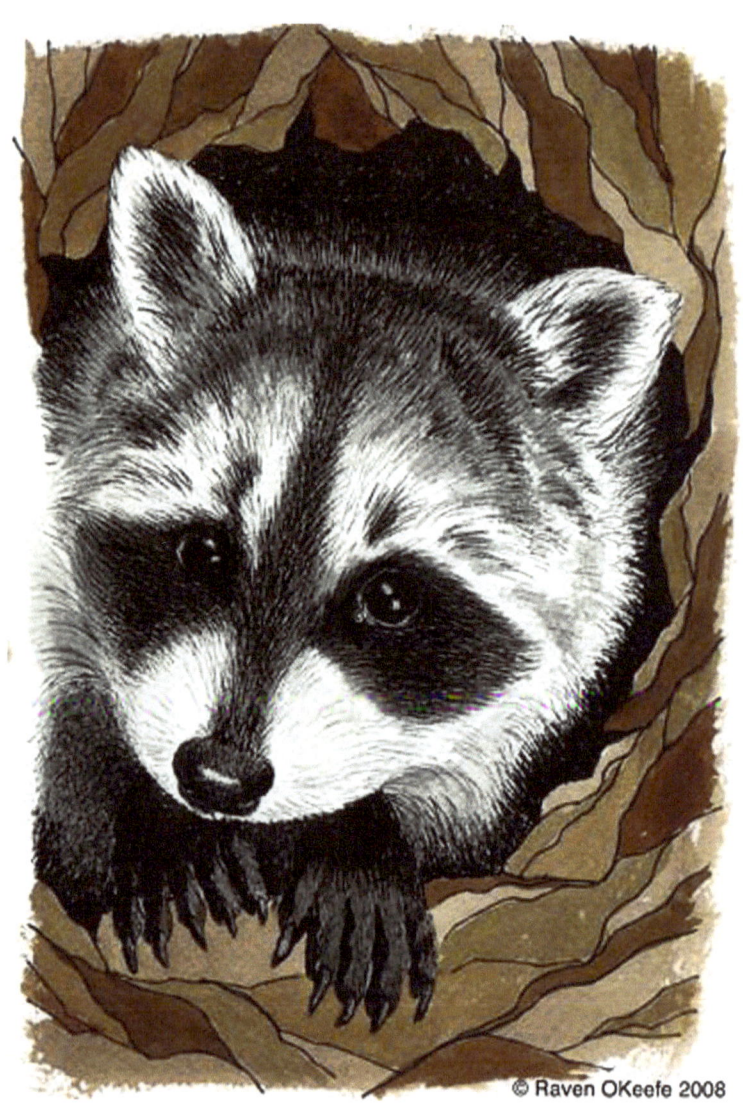

You knocked?

"I have spent my whole life learning and practicing my art. I've been drawing since I was old enough to hold a crayon and have been a full-time professional artist specializing in wildlife art and animal portraits for about 20 years.

"First I do the drawing with a special, very fine-pointed, artist's pen and permanent India ink. Then I color the piece with repeated layers of watercolor washes to give a rich, warm color to the artwork, adding a lifelike quality to the original drawing."

Raven

www.ingramcontent.com/pod-product-compliance
Lightning Source LLC
Chambersburg PA
CBHW040238220526
45473CB00001B/290